Mindfulness
as Mission Gift

KAREN OPENSHAW
&
CHRIS EDMONDSON

Copyright © 2022
Karen Openshaw & Chris Edmondson
All rights reserved.
ISBN: 9798406110003

Published by Fresh Expressions
www.freshexpressions.org.uk

COMMENDATIONS

"A really helpful resource.
The stories near the end alone are worth the money!"

Rev. Dr Michael Moynagh, co-author of
The 21st Century Christian: Following Jesus Where Life Happens.

"This booklet provides a wonderfully helpful and inspiring introduction to using mindfulness inside and outside church. Karen and Chris show how the current enthusiasm for this ancient practice of cultivating attentive presence is good news for all who are overwhelmed with busyness, stress, and exhaustion. They invite us to see how the practice of mindfulness has been threaded through the best of our faith tradition, from its earliest roots to its latest flowering. Their words encourage all of us to follow the pioneers of faith who felt called to go outside their comfort zone to listen and learn from other traditions in order to bring healing and wholeness to a broken world."

J M G Williams, FBA, Professor Emeritus of
Clinical Psychology, University of Oxford

CONTENTS

	Introduction	Pg 1
1	Making Connections	Pg 4
2	Where It All Begins: God's Mindfulness Of Us	Pg 8
3	Nothing New Under The Sun	Pg 12
4	Stories Of Mindfulness Practice	Pg 18
5	Why Offer Mindfulness As A Mission Gift?	Pg 25
6	What Next For You?	Pg 27
	Appendix: The Fresh Expressions Prayer	Pg 29
	Bibliography/Suggested Reading	Pg 30
	About the Authors	Pg 32

INTRODUCTION

This exploration into mindfulness as a mission gift seems to be timely in the light of the dreadful impact of Covid-19. There is growing evidence of people asking searching questions, not least about God and what Christianity has to offer amid so much heartache and uncertainty. We hope that what follows might offer some principles and practical examples as to how we, as church, can be a gift to our world in these challenging times. In what follows we seek to offer some insights for those wishing to incorporate mindful practices for the purposes of mission and to provide signposting to further resources. Mindful practice might shape our mission and be a means of introducing others to Jesus.

The fact that church buildings were initially closed for worship led to the development of "online church" much of which was more easily accessible to non-churchgoers or the spiritually seeking. There is evidence too, that the reach of the local church in serving its local communities, in culturally relevant ways, has increased significantly.

In her Grove publication *Mission in a Time of Trauma,* Rhona Knight opens with words from Tom Wright's *God and the Pandemic,* "These people, prayerful and humble, will be the answer ... to the question What? What needs to be done here? Who is most at risk? How can we help? Who shall we send? God works in all things *with and through* those who love him."[1]

One such example can be found at St Cuthbert's in Liverpool where they, under the leadership of Revd. Laura Leatherbarrow, have initiated an online 'Sanctuary' course. In this nine-week exploration of mental health, mindfulness sessions were delivered over Zoom tackling issues such as bipolar disorder, addiction, and suicide with separate sessions for under and over 13s. In the *Church Times*[2] Ms Leatherbarrow said "The young people who are 16 plus and just starting A levels find a way of taking back the control

---

[1] Tom Wright, *God and the Pandemic* (London: SPCK, 2020) pp 34-35.
[2] Church Times *Features,* 8 January 2021: www.churchtimes.co.uk/articles/2021/8-january/features/features/mental-ill-health-the-hidden-pandemic

they felt they had lost. The sessions allowed one lad to admit to his mum that he is depressed, and they have now made a GP appointment. One girl even attended a session while in hospital, because she wanted to keep a grip on the anxiety about missing schoolwork, and the effect that Covid has had on her life." They also plan to host a group using the 'Well-being Journey' course material (www.wellbeingjourney.org).

Many Christians are sceptical of mindfulness, so it is encouraging to know that the person recognised as the United Kingdom's leading authority on mindfulness is an Anglican priest! Mark Williams is also Emeritus Professor of Clinical Psychology and Honorary Senior Research Fellow at the University of Oxford's Department of Psychiatry, and we are grateful to him for his commendation of this publication.

The outline of this booklet is as follows:

In **Chapter 1** we share something of our respective journeys in coming to see mindfulness as a mission gift.

In **Chapter 2** we will explore mindfulness as an expression of the Missio Dei found in our Christian Scriptures and seen in the person and practice of Jesus.

Chapter 3 reminds us of the links to, and similarities between, mindfulness and the practices of Christians down the centuries which have had a powerful effect within and beyond the church in many different contexts.

Chapter 4 focuses on several examples of ways the insights of mindfulness are already proving to be a mission gift.

Chapters 5 and 6 offer suggestions on how to begin contextually applying the insights of mindfulness to engage missionally within our local communities.

However, firstly it is important to define mindfulness.

Present day mindfulness has its roots in the work of Jon Kabat-Zinn, a professor of medicine who, in the 1970's, developed a meditation-based programme, known as Mindfulness Based Stress Reduction, aimed at helping to support people suffering from chronic pain, stress and illness. Tim Stead comments "Kabat-Zinn had learned meditation techniques from Buddhist teachers but will always argue that it was not the religious aspects of meditation which interested him, but the health value of the practices themselves."[3]

The field has been further developed particularly through the work of three clinical scientists, specialists in cognitive therapy: Mark Williams, (to whom reference has already been made), Zindel Segal and John Teasdale.

Dictionary definitions of mindfulness include the following:

"The quality or state of being conscious or aware of something."

"A mental state achieved by focusing one's awareness on the present moment, while calmly acknowledging and accepting one's feelings, thoughts and bodily sensations, used as a therapeutic technique."[4]

Jon Kabat-Zinn describes mindfulness as "Awareness that arises through paying attention, on purpose, in the present moment, non-judgementally, and then I sometimes add, in the service of self-understanding and wisdom."[5]

---

[3] Tim Stead, *Mindfulness and Prayer* (Cambridge: Grove Books Ltd, 2016) p2.
[4] https://www.lexico.com/definition/mindfulness
[5] https://www.mindful.org/jon-kabat-zinn-defining-mindfulness/

1 MAKING CONNECTIONS

Speaking of and demonstrating God's love to a broken, hurting world means discovering a language people can understand and which finds expression in a meaningful and accessible way. To connect people outside the church to God is an act of the imagination especially in the case of those who do not profess a faith.

Over the centuries, many people have wrestled with how to make connections with, or build bridges to, faith in challenging circumstances. To set the scene we begin with two examples from the Acts of the Apostles. In addition, there are insights from a book which has been important for both of us. This will be followed by stories from our own respective journeys which have enabled us to see how mindfulness can prove to be a mission gift and may have the potential to become a fresh expression of church.

Making connections in the Acts of the Apostles

In Acts chapter 16, following a vision, Paul and Silas find themselves in the city of Philippi in Macedonia. They go to what is described as a "place of prayer" and meet up with Lydia and other women. From Luke's account, these people were "spiritually open" and already engaging in some form of prayer. Paul and Silas gain the trust of this group of women by listening and being present, alert, and respectful. Luke tells us "The Lord opened her [Lydia's] heart to listen eagerly to what was said by Paul" (Acts 16:14) and she became the first person to be baptised in Europe.

Following on from this Paul is in Athens, distressed by his experience of this city "full of idols" he is given the opportunity to speak at a meeting of the Areopagus [City Council]. His address is a model of listening, engaging, and communicating with a very different culture. Paul uses examples they understood from their own context. He then establishes common ground by emphasising what they agree on about God. Only after this did he speak of Christ, centring on the resurrection. In his recent book[6], Michael Moynagh

---

[6] Moynagh, M. and Beck, M. *The 21st Century Christian: Following Jesus Where Life*

illustrates a model of creating a fresh expression of church which begins with this kind of listening and loving.

At the heart of Paul's address was his recognition of the spiritual searching of the Athenians, especially as he refers to the altar he spotted with the inscription "TO AN UNKNOWN GOD." His response was "What you worship as something unknown, I am going to proclaim to you." (Acts 17: 23).

Paul's address received a mixed reaction with some sneering, some wanting to know more, and a few responding positively in the moment. Had he used his "synagogue approach," reciting Jewish history and speaking of Jesus as the fulfilment of Messianic prophecies, it would have fallen on deaf ears. Through listening and respecting them and being alert to the promptings of the Holy Spirit, Paul took the risk of entering a different culture and thereby helped people make connections, which for some became life-changing for all involved.

Insights from *Christianity Rediscovered.*

Vincent Donovan's *Christianity Rediscovered* is a seminal and prophetic book, and over the last forty years it has become a well-known story. Donovan, a Roman Catholic priest working in East Africa, abandoned traditional missionary methods where mission work had been largely based in buildings, through establishing hospitals and schools. Although the work had been valuable, he became conscious that there was little evidence of this missional approach bringing people to God. Considering this, Donovan engaged with the Masai in a very different way: on their territory, living with, listening to, learning from, and eating with them.

The relevance of this for us is that Donovan assumed no preconceived notions of God, Christ, salvation, or anything traditionally associated with Christianity. Instead, through intentional listening and being present with and respectful of (mindful of) the Masai people and their culture, he began to find a language and approach which enabled him to share the message of Christ with those who had either never heard of, or did not believe in, him.

Connections for Chris

I first read *Christianity Rediscovered* in 1984 as a vicar of a challenging inner-urban parish in West Yorkshire. We were about to plant a new congregation

---

Happens. A Fresh Expressions book, 2021

in one of the two large social housing estates that made up most of the parish. Although ministry among the Masai of Tanzania, and the people of north Halifax might seem to have nothing in common, some of the principles enshrined in *Christianity Rediscovered*, helped to shape what became a very different approach to being church. As a church we listened, prayed, and tried to find a new language with which to communicate and express God's love and, indeed, his "mindfulness" of and care for the people of those very needy and broken communities.

Twelve years later, as a vicar in Bradford, a priority became a small, rather forgotten area of social housing within the parish. Despite attempts over the years to connect with the people who lived there, few from the estate ever became part of the parish church. Once again, keeping in mind the principles from *Christianity Rediscovered* we tried to listen - both to God and to the needs of the area. We visited each house on the estate to ask what might enhance the quality of life there, and how we, as a church, could contribute to this. This resulted in a new presence on the estate known as 'The Source'.[7]

As I reflect, many years on, I sense that both mission initiatives could have benefited from the practice of mindfulness - had we known of such a thing. But I do believe that we were "mindful" in our approach as we listened, we accepted what was "in the present moment" and we acknowledged previous unhelpful approaches.

Connections for Karen

In 2012, as part of my role at the Oasis Academy in Salford (OAMCUK) as chaplain and church leader, I had been tasked with establishing a fresh expression of church. This was something that proved exciting and challenging although personally costly. I was introduced to the Vincent Donovan text as part of my training. It proved invaluable in helping to form what church in that context should look like. It was more about listening to, and then meeting the needs of, a community which was in the top percentile for disadvantage and poverty in the country, despite being juxtaposed with the wealthy Media City UK - the new home of the BBC in the North.

In early 2017, after receiving a diagnosis of fibromyalgia, it was suggested to me that I attend an 8-week secular mindfulness course. My teacher was Martin Grindrod (www.inspiremindfulness.co.uk) who was, at that time, a 'de-churched' Christian who had learned mindfulness through a Buddhist-

---

[7] For more details of the story see *Mission-shaped church* (London: Church House Publishing, 2004, Seventh impression 2005) pp 58-59.

based organisation (www.breathworks-mindfulness.org.uk). He is now closely involved in local church with a re-ignited faith. Many Christians think of mindfulness as a Buddhist practice but, through my work for the consultancy I set up in 2016 (www.karenopenshaw.co.uk) I discovered there were many connections between mindfulness and the spiritual disciplines I already practised. I realised the potential there might be in offering mindfulness and meditation practice as part of the Church's mission. It would certainly have been a blessing to me, and for those with whom I engaged with through my role at OAMCUK. I realise now that many of the initiatives I set up were in fact mindfulness based.

Furthermore, I believe practising mindfulness and meditation, alongside my faith, would have prevented some of the burnouts that, as a pioneer, I experienced, and I am passionate about sharing its value with people of all faiths and none. As Sheridan Voysey has expressed it in his blog *Six Ways to Tend Your Soul in Times of Turmoil*, "As important as mindfulness techniques have been found to be .... we also need strength from outside us, especially as we go forward in these difficult days."[8] For me, and I would suggest for all Christians, this strength comes from God.

Connections through the Nazareth manifesto

Research has shown that becoming mindful, and the practice of meditation, changes the neural pathways in the brain and calms the amygdala. This in turn brings about feelings of peace and increased well-being. We would connect this sense of life taking on a new and fresh perspective with the gift at the very heart of Jesus' mission as summed up in Luke 4: 18-19, and fulfilling the Messianic prophecy found in Isaiah 61:1-2.

"The Spirit of the Lord is on me, because he has anointed me to proclaim good news to the poor. He has sent me to proclaim freedom for the prisoners and recovery of sight for the blind, to set the oppressed free, to proclaim the year of the Lord's favour."

We play our part in bringing about lasting change for individuals and society by joining Jesus where he is already at work. We need, as suggested in the examples above, to continually be alert to God working in new ways and making fresh connections. We do this through experimenting and exploring, by praying and listening to what the Spirit might be saying, by being present and mindful to the needs of others and loving those he puts alongside us.

---

[8] https://sheridanvoysey.com/tending-your-soul-in-times-of-turmoil/ - date accessed 11/01/22.

2 WHERE IT ALL BEGINS: GOD'S MINDFULNESS OF US

"When I look at the heavens, the work of your fingers, the moon, and stars that you have established; what are human beings that you are mindful of them, mortals that you care for them?" (Psalm 8:4 NRSV)

Scanning the night sky, the Psalmist - in this instance King David - is awed by the immensity and vastness of creation, and asks God (and himself) this profound question, 'Why does the Creator of all this beauty and wonder, have his mind full of humanity?'

The answer unfolds in a subsequent verse which describes how the heavens and humans alike are made by the same loving creator. The psalmist continues to say that God has made humans "a little lower than the angels and crowned them with glory and honour." (Psalm 8: 5 NIV)

This should not surprise us because going back to the creation story in Genesis 1, verse 27 tells us that "God created humankind in his own image, in the image of God he created them; male and female he created them." When God formed us, he had himself in mind. We were created to be like him in spirit, our bodies being vessels to express this truth. The fall may have marred this image and likeness, but it has not destroyed it. We are *still* named, known, and valued (Psalm 139).

The word 'Enos' in the Hebrew translates as "human beings/frail mortal" not "Adam" which means humankind as a whole. 'Enos' by contrast, means an individual person. There are further examples of the word translated as "mindful," as well as of God's implicit mindfulness woven through the Christian Scriptures. Including:

"He will ever be **mindful** of his Covenant." (Psalm 111:5)

"The Lord has been **mindful** of us; he will bless us." (Psalm 115: 12)

"For he himself knows our frame; he is **mindful** that we are but dust." (Psalm 103:14).

Other uses of the word are found in Psalms 144:3; 40:17; 136:23; and Job 7:17.

In his book, *A Book of Sparks: A Study in Christian MindFullness,* Shaun Lambert writes: "In the Greek Septuagint version of the Old Testament, the word used is 'mimneske' - to be mindful of, to actively remember. There is a high level of personal involvement in the remembering that is mindfulness, the involvement of our awareness and attention."[9]

God's mindfulness of humanity, and how we seek to live out of that, is a vital message to convey in contemporary society.

The mindfulness of Jesus

In his interactions with others

Reading the Gospels through the lens of the 'mindful Jesus' we discover that he was always fully present, in the moment to God, others, and himself. Such mindfulness meant he was able to make the right choices and not give in to the pressures and expectations of others, real or imagined.

He saw in ways that others often did not. In the Gospels the word translated into English as 'seeing' occurs forty times. Jesus' 'seeing' was almost always as a result of being moved with compassion, often for the benefit of the marginalised.

Many who saw Jesus call Zaccheus down from the tree (Luke 19:7) and go to his house, were shocked and offended. Yet Jesus saw him, showed him compassion, and only *then* challenged him to change.

Further examples of Jesus' 'seeing' include the encounter with the woman who had been bleeding for many years. She had been isolated and ostracised and touched the hem of his robe in desperation. Jesus said "Someone touched me. I know that power has gone out from me" (Luke 8: 46). Clearly, Jesus was in tune with his body and mindful of the needs of the woman in that moment, even though others may have seen this as an interruption to his schedule. Luke 18:35-43 is another such example.

Mindfulness also involves paying attention to our own feelings (non-judgementally). In the Garden of Gethsemane, Jesus says "My soul is

---

[9] Shaun Lambert, *A Book of Sparks: A Study in Christian MindFullness* (Watford: Instant Apostle, 2014) p35.

overwhelmed with sorrow to the point of death" (Mark 14:34). He owned both the sense of emotional anxiety and the physical signs his body was sending him in that moment, as well as being mindful of what lay ahead of him.

In his teaching

From Jesus' teaching in the Sermon on the Mount two examples stand out.

Firstly, in Matthew 6:25-34 Jesus addresses our human propensity to worry, a message relevant for every generation and context, not least our own in the light of Covid-19. As already stated, there is scientific evidence that practising mindfulness changes the anatomy of the brain reducing symptoms of anxiety and depression.

The second is in Matthew 7:1-5. Given that mindfulness encourages a non-judgemental attitude to ourselves and others, Jesus' words here are very pertinent. He tells us to carefully examine our motives, words, and conduct, before judging others: specks and planks! This is a call to be self-aware and discerning and invites an attitude of kindness and compassion, including to self.

Mindfulness also helps us apply the teaching of Jesus by learning to 'be' in the present moment. In Matthew 6 this involves addressing the issue of control; instead of concentrating our attention on the fantasies and catastrophes our minds create we 'come to our senses' - the phrase used of the younger son in the Parable of the Father with two sons (Luke 15:17).

Writing in *World Mission Magazine,* Catholic Psychologist Gregory Bottaro cites Jean Pierre de Caussade's classic *Abandonment to Divine Providence* when he says, "What makes the Christian's experience of the present moment unique, as Fr. de Caussade reminds us, is the awareness that God is a loving Father who keeps us constantly in His loving care. While our life is an unfolding of reality that is perceived in our minds as taking place over time, in God's mind it occurs as one present moment."[10]

Commenting on this in an article in the *Church Times,* David Bryant writes "This homes in on the concept of mindfulness, that is having a resurrection at present. It is the process by which we evaluate each moment, drawing from

---

[10] https://worldmissionmagazine.com/archives/wm-march-2020/christian-approach-mindfulness

it a deeper more acute awareness of its consistency and meaning."[11]

Modelled for others

The Gospels, especially Mark and Luke, clearly show that in order to be present and engaged in his public ministry, Jesus intentionally practised the spiritual disciplines of reflection, prayer, fasting and solitude.

Jesus would go to a quiet place, to be with his Heavenly Father and be 'reminded' of how much he was loved, along with seeking guidance. Jesus perfectly modelled contemplative activism and sought to instil that in his disciples.

After their first exciting but demanding experience of evangelism, "The apostles gathered around Jesus and reported to him all they had done and taught. Then, because so many people were coming and going that they did not even have a chance to eat, he said to them, 'Come with me by yourselves to a quiet place and get some rest.' So they went away by themselves in a boat to a solitary place." (Mark 6: 30-32)

The word here for 'rest' in the original Greek of the New Testament is 'anapauo,' which conveys the meaning of rest involving body, mind, and spirit. The 'mindful Jesus' offers the model for this through his life and example. We engage with and minister to the needs, anxieties and hopes of life in the world today by having "the same mindset as Christ Jesus" (Philippians 2:5).

---

[11] https://www.churchtimes.co.uk/articles/2016/1-april/faith/faith-features/present-in-this-moment

3 NOTHING NEW UNDER THE SUN

In Ecclesiastes 1:9, we read "What has been is what will be, and what has been done is what will be done; there is nothing new under the sun." These words seem very apt when it comes to the relationship between mindfulness and the Christian tradition. The word itself may have appeared in the latter part of the 20th century, and initially been associated with the Buddhist religion, but much of what is at the heart of mindfulness has been practised by Christians for centuries. The mindful Christian aspires to a conscious awareness of the presence of God in all situations.

"We haven't called it mindfulness. We've called it 'silent prayer' or 'contemplative prayer,' 'the desert tradition,' or 'mystical theology,' but it has been there from Jesus, through St Paul, all the way up to the present."[12]

We have already alluded to seeing Jesus' life and ministry through the lens of mindfulness. You could say the contemplative tradition began with Jesus, through his example and teaching. As well as Jesus' own attentiveness to his Father, others, and himself, he constantly tells his disciples to have "eyes to see and ears to hear."

Mindfulness and St Paul

Without reading mindfulness into every text in Scripture we find further encouragements to be mindful, in the writings of St Paul.

Examples include:

"For who has known the mind of the Lord so as to instruct him? But we have the mind of Christ" (1 Corinthians 2: 16).

"You were taught to be ... renewed in the spirit of your minds" (Ephesians 4:23).

---

[12] Tim Stead, *Mindfulness in the Christian tradition*, https://chreader.org/mindfulness-christian-tradition

"Finally, beloved, whatever is true, whatever is honourable, whatever is just, whatever is pure, whatever is pleasing, whatever is commendable, if there is any excellence, and if there is anything worthy of praise, think about these things" (Philippians 4: 8).

"Do not be conformed to this world, but be transformed by the renewal of your minds, so that you may discern what is the will or God - what is good, acceptable, and perfect" (Romans 12:2).

At the 2020 Christian Mindfulness Conference, Amy Oden, Professor of Early Church History at St Paul School of Theology in Kansas, observed that the Message version of the following words from Romans, "sound like a great description of Christian mindfulness".

"Take your everyday, ordinary life - your sleeping, eating, going-to-work and walking around life - and place it before God ... You'll be changed from the inside out" (Romans 12:2 *The Message*)[13].

She went on to say that "The call to be mindful of our lives, 'placed before God' rings through every Christian century ... Christian mindfulness is simply paying attention to our lives held within God's life."[14] And the purpose of becoming mindful for a Christian is to outwork this in our interactions with others.

A flavour of mindfulness down the centuries...

The common thread running through the following examples is that they practised mindfulness of God in order to better engage missionally with the world.

St Anthony spearheaded a movement in the 3rd century that became known as the **Desert Fathers and Mothers**. These were men and women, (the women known as 'ammas,' meaning spiritual mothers), who, becoming concerned about the growing worldliness of the church, went to live as hermits in the Scetes desert of Egypt where they later formed communities. Their experience led them to describe prayer as "the active work of laying aside our thoughts," through the practice of 'apatheia' - paying attention, and by making themselves open and available to God.

---

[13] Eugene H. Peterson, *The Message,* (Used by permission of NavPress. Tyndale House Publishers, Inc. © 1993, 2002, 2018).

[14] https://www.spst.edu/inside-out-an-invitation-to-christian-mindfulness/

Part of our reason for believing this is a timely opportunity (Kairos moment) to connect mindfulness and mission, comes from the way many in our own day are turning to mindfulness, as they experience the stresses and strains of modern life. In a way this has parallels with the thousands in the third and fourth centuries who flocked to the desert, to see if they could find something different and deeper which connected with their day to day lives, other than in the ways the then 'institutional church' was offering.

St Augustine, (AD 354-430), described prayer as 'the way to mind-fullness', and spoke of the connections between attention and self-awareness.

St. Benedict, (AD 480-547) is widely regarded as the founder of Western monasticism. His 'Rule' of monastic life is a rhythm of prayer and work (Ora et Labora), where monks were encouraged to bring their mindfulness to God amid daily life. They were in all things 're-minded' of God. This remains one of the most influential rules in monastic life today.

In, *A Book of Sparks,* Shaun Lambert quotes these words from the Rule of Benedict, "One must 'flee forgetfulness' and always be mindful of what God has commanded (Rule of Benedict 7 :10-11)."[15]

He goes on to say, "So at the heart of the Christian scaffolding for mindfulness within a Benedictine understanding is an awareness of the presence of God and remembering to translate into action what God wants us to do."[16]

St Ignatius Loyola (1491-1556). His 'Examen' is an invitation to be mindfully present to God and self by taking time to reflect on the presence and activity of God through the events and people of the day. This is a discipline many today are rediscovering, which includes prayer for light to understand and appreciate the day that has passed, reviewing the day with thanksgiving, and reflecting and praying on feelings experienced as the day is replayed.

Teresa of Avila (1515-1582) is especially remembered for her method of prayer, referred to as "the prayer of recollection." This can be summarised as intentionally taking time for slow, attentive prayer as a means of taking the pray-er deeper into their relationship with God.

---

[15] Lambert, 2014, p36-7
[16] Lambert, 2014, p37.

Brother Lawrence - Nicholas Herman, of Lorraine (1614-1691). His spiritual classic, *The Practice of the Presence of God* closely connects with some of the insights of mindfulness. At the heart of the conversations and letters collected in this book, is a commitment to developing the practice of being attentive to the presence of God, whether engaged in domestic chores or other work, looking after children or meeting with friends. In other words, no sacred-secular divide or escapist other-worldly kind of spirituality. Rather, we see lived out here, a call to living an integrated life. That is, living the ordinary, everyday life mindfully and prayerfully. Again, we suggest, a relevant message to the searching and longings of many in today's world; particularly those who might describe themselves as spiritual.

John Wesley (1703-1791). Wesley is best known as the leader of a revival movement known as Methodism. This word was initially used in general terms to describe the methodical way in which Wesley, his brother Charles and other early leaders approached their discipleship within the Anglican Church. Later, however, he used the word to describe the methodical pursuit of Biblical holiness including 'watchfulness', being mindful in all situations of what we think, say, and do. He took his preaching from the building out to the people.

The 19th century, especially through the Oxford Movement, saw the beginnings of a revival of the monastic life for men and women in England. These took various expressions and included several new orders committed to the twin priorities of contemplation and action. This was demonstrated through living and working in some of the most deprived and challenging communities in the United Kingdom. One example is the Community of the Resurrection located in Industrial West Yorkshire.

During the 20th and 21st centuries, certain figures have challenged and reminded the church of its calling to both contemplation and action. Among these are the French mystic, **Simone Weil**, **Evelyn Underhill**, Trappist monk **Thomas Merton**, **Henri Nouwen** and **John Main**, founder of the World Community for Christian Meditation. Mindfulness, in Main's teaching, is expressed as a way of preparing and recollecting in order to be able to fully focus on God. He says, "We must collect ourselves together. We must become mindful, remember who we are and where we are and why we are. We need to find a peace within ourselves and a peace in our lives. This peace is mindfulness."[17]

Richard Rohr. For many today, the writings of this Franciscan Friar,

---

[17] John Main, *The Heart of Creation* (London DLT, 1988) p83

founder of the Centre for Action and Contemplation, have become a significant means by which these two callings, seen lived out perfectly in the person of Jesus, can be held together in the vicissitudes of daily living. In one of his 2020 daily reflections he wrote this,

"'Let the same mind be in you that was in Christ Jesus,' (Philippians 2:5). How do we put on the mind of Christ? How do we see through his eyes? How do we feel through his heart? How do we learn to respond to the world with that same wholeness and healing love? That's what Christian orthodoxy is really all about. It's not just about right belief; it's about right practice."[18]

Different strands; same source and aim

We would suggest that all these strands of spirituality, in their different ways, share a common foundation in their focus: the personal experiencing of God's presence with us, here and now in this moment, learning to be present in all things, and to all things. In this sense, mindfulness of and with God could be described as the taproot of prayer. And flowing from this should come the desire to "proclaim freedom for the prisoners and recovery of sight for the blind, to set the oppressed free" (Luke 4:18).

It is important to trace this rich Christian heritage, which is often either unknown to, or overlooked by, those who may be drawn to mindfulness. Sadly, this can be because it is only Eastern religions which are seen as capable of responding to, or connecting with, a transcendent reality in contrast with what has been described as "the sheer verbiage of so much Christian worship and prayer." Or as novelist E.M. Forster expressed it in his novel *A Passage to India*, "poor talkative little Christianity!"[19]

Christian meditation and contemplative practice are self-evidently diverse. The distinction of Christian mindfulness from any other model, is that mindfulness is understood as being primarily the prerogative of God who is, first and foremost, mindful of us and graciously invites us into relationship with him through the gift of his Son. Knowing this can help us to explore how we might make connections with those who are not aware of this. Knowing this can help us to explore how we might make connections with those who are not aware of this

---

[18] Centre for Action and Contemplation, *The Kingdom as Consciousness*, (Wednesday November 18th, 2020) cac.org.
[19] E M Forster, *A Passage to India*, (London: Penguin Classics, 1924. This edition 2005), Chapter 14.

In the article *Inside Out: An Invitation to Christian Mindfulness,* Amy Oden writes "We have a deep well of theologies and spiritual practices, and it's important to add that we have taken wrong turns and learned to repent, again and again. Yet throughout it all, God has been mindful of us. God reaches out to all people in all places, with an invitation to relationship."[20]

We need to be wary of making any false distinction suggesting mindful meditation is self-focused, whereas Christian meditation is God focused. If the purpose of any approach to meditation or contemplation is seen only as a quick fix for the reduction of stress and tension this might be the case. But rightly understood, mindfulness practices can support and enable, life changing encounters. For example, when using breathing exercises, and reciting a mantra from the Scriptures like 'Maranatha,' or the Jesus Prayer ("Lord Jesus Christ, Son of God, have mercy on me a sinner") the nature of the Christian's encounter, is with God.

I (Karen) would add that in the work I do offering a listening service, where the employees of an organisation can share their worries and concerns, I have observed a marked difference between how people of faith have been coping with the challenges of life during the Coronavirus pandemic. None of us are immune from anxiety, but through being aware of the God who is mindful of us, especially in times of great uncertainty, it is possible to experience as Jesus promised, "a peace that the world cannot give" (John 14:27).

To meditate, to contemplate, to listen, to imagine, to sit in silence is, we suggest, to practise being mindful. These are means of both enabling and deepening a relationship with God, along with a greater non-judging self-awareness, and compassion for others.

We believe meditative and mindful practices are sanctifying, peace-making, hunger-satisfying and part of what the Church can offer and model to a world crying out for stillness, depth, and serenity: in the truest sense, they are evangelistic.

---

[20] https://www.spst.edu/inside-out-an-invitation-to-christian-mindfulness/

4 STORIES OF MINDFULNESS PRACTICE

In this chapter, we will cite examples of individuals and churches who have used insights from mindfulness and meditation as a mission gift and, in some instances, to shape a fresh expression of church.

The term 'fresh expressions' first appeared as part of the Church of England's 2004 Report, *Mission-Shaped Church: Church Planting and Fresh Expressions of Church in a Changing Context*. The word 'fresh' comes from the Church of England's 'Declaration of Assent,' which includes the phrase "which faith the church is called upon to proclaim afresh, in each generation."

A fresh expression of church has been described as "a new Christian gathering developed mainly for the benefit of people who are not yet members of any church. Fresh expressions listen to those outside the church, and enter their culture, to help them meet and follow Jesus in an environment that is comfortable and relevant to them."[21]

The fresh expressions journey involves listening, loving, serving, building community, exploring discipleship, church taking shape, and then doing it again, seeing these ingredients as a helpful framework, not as linear.

The many fresh expressions which have emerged in the years since the *Mission-Shaped Church* report, take varied forms but have key values in common. They are missional, contextual, formational, and ecclesial (www.freshexpressions.org.uk).

What follows is a deliberately eclectic mix. Some are about intentional, compassionate missional engagement; others may feel the phrase 'mindful church' describes them.

Community engagement in Leicestershire

Whilst working as a Community Centre leader in Leicestershire, Baptist

---

[21] '*Fresh Expressions and Pioneer Ministry*', www.leeds.anglican.org/fresh-expressions

minister Sue Steer regularly engaged in conversation with members of a mental health support group who used the building. Based on her own experience of finding contemplative prayer and meditation to be helpful and calming, Sue asked this group if they would be interested in exploring this for themselves. They began to use forms of guided meditation that were not explicitly Christian but had references to Jesus within them.

From there, they began to explore mindfulness and started to use some of its techniques in their meditation group. After some months, members of the group began to discuss what faith meant to them. Eventually, this led to them becoming a Christian meditation group, which incorporated insights from mindfulness.

Sue moved in 2019 to another role as a pioneer community worker in a new housing estate in Lubbesthorpe, Leicestershire. She trained as a mindfulness teacher and offers six-week courses for people of all faiths and none, which, due to the Coronavirus pandemic, currently take place on Zoom. She also offers specifically Christian mindfulness courses.

Mindfulness workshops

Through my consultancy, I (Karen), offer introduction to mindfulness workshops for secular organisations, in order to help equip people to live more mindfully. These sessions are designed for people of all faiths and none, and do not have any explicit spiritual or religious content. However, I am able to share some of my own practices of Christian mindfulness and meditation and end the sessions with a "kindness" verse which those of faith would identify as a prayer, and others as a mantra.

From the responses I have received, it would suggest that there is enormous potential for local churches to offer similar kinds of sessions within their communities, particularly to benefit those struggling with poor mental health. This might also provide a platform to create a specific mindful fresh expression of church.

I also offer workshops for Christian organisations to remind them of the importance of being mindful of the presence of God.

Sacred Space is a fresh expression of church in Kingston, within the Diocese of Southwark. This is led by Andrea Campanale, a lay pioneer working for the Church Mission Society. This grew out of a piece of work with spiritual seekers at fairs and community events. Using the arts and Christ-centred spiritual practices, including mindfulness, interactive prayer spaces are created through which people can encounter God.

Two related initiatives are:

Deep - a six-week meditation course at the YMCA in nearby Surbiton, run by members of Sacred Space. All the leaders were Christians, but the various meditation practices and spiritual exercises were accessible to people of any or no faith.

SpiritSpace - a transatlantic project which came out of the virtual Burning Man Festival in August 2020. A monthly on-line gathering for 'the spiritual not religious', this uses mindfulness meditations and creative reflections in the main room and offers prayer ministry and waiting on the Holy Spirit in the breakout rooms.

St George's C of E Church in Worcester offer an opportunity on the evening of the third Sunday of every month to pause, using Scripture in a mindful way to help people focus or refocus on God more clearly. The sessions begin with silence, moving into short mindfulness practices. A Bible passage or verse is read, followed by a reflection using the words from the passage. There may sometimes be a guided reflection. After each practice, people can share their own responses if they wish. There are also free audio downloads available.

Mindful Moments takes place each Tuesday morning at the Methodist Hub in Milnthorpe, Cumbria. This takes the form of a relaxed drop-in session, with M:Hub's café open for coffee and chat along with a space in the adjoining room to be part of a meditative activity, in order to enable people to find some stillness amid a busy day.

Building on this, the church has organised a series of 'Explore Mindfulness' sessions, led by someone who is both a social worker and pioneer minister for the Methodist Church. The publicity for these sessions includes the following:

"Mindfulness has lots to teach Christians on our faith journey. Not only does it help to reduce stress and anxiety, but also gives us fresh perspectives on the love of God, compassion, and forgiveness. We will be exploring mindfulness meditation and techniques together, and finding out more about how it helps stress, anxiety, and our spiritual lives."[22]

---

[22] https://www.kendalmethodistcircuit.org.uk/explore-mindfulness-from-a-christian-perspective/

Focus ran from 2015 to 2017 in La Tour Cycle Cafe in Ipswich, Suffolk. This contemplative meditation group grew out of various conversations between the Revd Tim Yau and those he met at Mind, Body and Spirit fairs, where he offered 'Soul Space,' an approach designed to engage with 'spiritual seekers'.

The sessions involved relaxation techniques, reflections on words of Scripture or spiritual writers, meditation, and reflection time/group feedback. Themes taken included: 'the fruits of the Spirit', 'together searching for the divine', 'catching the divine voice', and 'Living Lent: discovering the divine in the wilderness'. They also tried the practice of Lectio Divina.

Over the time Focus was in existence its weekly meetings would attract 8 to 10 people, with 30 on the mailing list. Attendees were diverse in age, background, and world view.

Meditation in Oakham

Since 2017, a long standing ecumenical Christian meditation group introduced a more intentional missional focus when they offered an evening class for the staff of a local employer, enabling many who were stressed to have an opportunity over eight weeks to learn the basic skills of Christian-rooted mindful meditation. They also approached a local primary school who invited them to teach meditation to Key Stage 2 classes. This led to some of the teachers leading short mindfulness sessions at other times in the week and meditation permeating the school culture. Iain Ramsey, reflects that the openness on the part of the schools to this, came because of two things: long-standing church links with schools, and signs of improvement in children's mental health. Might we suggest that these are signs of the kingdom beginning to break in?

Mindful Breakfast and Forest Church

In 2014, Lynsey Heslegrave established a new pioneer church community which began by holding a monthly Mindful Prayer breakfast. This was part of a vision to establish a community committed to listening to and being more attentive to God. Those who gathered were a mixture of established church members, individuals 'burnt out' on established church, others who had faith but were 'dechurched', and yet others were brought by friends.

Lynsey also developed a monthly Forest Church enabling people to learn how to be 'more present' within creation and provided fresh insights on reading and engaging with Scripture by using meditative and mindful processes by learning to be 'in the moment' and not to be over-attached to thoughts and feelings.

Positive changes were observed in those attending by people who knew them. Even though lockdown has prevented further developments, the core group are continuing to practise mindful prayer via Zoom and potential exists for developing and growing this.

Mindful Church Café was led by the Revd Shaun Lambert and ran on a regular basis at Costa in Stanmore, Middlesex from October 2014 to April 2018. Their strapline was 'mindfulness for health, and mindfulness of God'. It was set up as an expression of contemplative evangelism aimed at reaching people in the surrounding community. Numbers varied from 6 to 30, some of whom had become aware of this initiative through the local 'healing on the streets' ministry. Themes included overtly Christian ones such as 'Jesus as sage - exploring a mindful path to wisdom', but also focussed on bridge-building topics such as stress, anxiety, parenting, grief, and loss - all from the perspective of mindfulness for health and God.

In terms of pattern and content, typically after refreshments there would be a mindful walk, interactive teaching, reflection, and meditation. The plan had been to run this on a weekly basis as a fresh expression of church in a neutral third space, but this proved to be difficult as managers of Costa kept changing.

A further initiative from Stanmore Baptist Church was to trial mindful church café sessions in their church car park, around a mobile coffee van - perhaps more suitable in the summer months!

Leeds Methodist Mission (LMM) is a City Centre project focused on reflection, wellbeing, activism, and creativity. They seek to create spaces and resources online and in person, for people to connect more deeply with themselves, one another, and on important issues of social justice. To enable this, opportunities are given to explore topics such as mindfulness, meditation, craftivism, well-being, climate change, Christian spirituality and much more. Anna Bland says the work is constantly evolving.

The Blackbird Project. Working with the Leeds Methodist Mission, this was initiated by the Huddersfield Methodist circuit in 2014. The aim was to work outside the church and help people whose mental health was suffering by offering safe relationships. After a year of research, the pioneer minister Tim Moore, began to teach mindfulness courses to members of the public. The decision to use village halls instead of church buildings was taken to help people feel more comfortable and to make mindfulness accessible to as many as possible. Part of the intention was to give those who suffered from low mood and stress tools for self-help, especially when they had to wait a lengthy time for clinical support and talking therapies. It was a gift from the Methodist church to anybody who wanted to come along, with courses delivered at a fraction of the usual cost. Early aims of delivering mindfulness and to explore spirituality were dropped in favour of letting participants find their own level. It was a project driven by those who attended rather than Tim or the circuit. This proved to be a risk well worth taking as many on the courses were keen to pursue more mindfulness and seek out a 'more spiritual way of life' without prompting.

The project continues to gather people and explore different ways of connecting with those outside of church via listening, bereavement listening, and wellbeing courses. Mindfulness has been an inspired choice as it is easily taught and, with practice, easily learnt. It is becoming normal for schools to teach and practice mindfulness and it is embedded in some NHS treatments as well as a range of clinical therapies. The Blackbird Project continues to use mindfulness because it is now a familiar concept to society and has proved effective.

Mindful church online ... the future?

Shaun Lambert has begun trialling online mindful church which, in his words, "subverts the virtual world by encouraging people into their body, senses and soul in their sitting rooms."[23]

Our final example comes from Scargill House, the Christian Community conference and retreat centre in the Yorkshire Dales. They began running Quiet days online during the early part of the pandemic in 2020 when it was not possible to be open to residential guests. These, along with retreat weekends on the theme of mindfulness, and other similar courses have had a high uptake. This shows the potential for offering more contemplative and mindful material online in order to engage with those for whom inherited church does not connect. Inherited church and fresh expressions of church could learn from this model and replicate.

Some questions on which to reflect.

The examples above have been descriptive rather than analytical. Here are a few questions to consider arising from them:

---

[23] Spoken in a conversation with Chris Edmondson in 2021

- Regardless of the nature of the initiative, does it play a part in serving the mission of God?

- Some of the above initiatives were quite short-lived. Why might this be? Is there value in short-term initiatives? Or was this because of inadequate planning or some other reason? How can the benefits of a short-term initiative be celebrated and not viewed as failure?

- Although it is not wrong to build an initiative around an individual, does over-dependence on the leader/pioneer affect the success of the project? Should there be a team approach from the start?

- What lessons might be learned about the importance of context: the how, when, and where of meeting?

- What other considerations should there be before establishing a new project?

- As community forms, what might the next steps be to explore discipleship?

- What might church look like in this context?

- In what ways are these examples a mission gift?

5 WHY OFFER MINDFULNESS AS A MISSION GIFT?

It may be that our only focus on offering mindfulness as a mission gift is to minister to people's wellbeing: physical, mental, and emotional because that is what Jesus would do. However, building upon this, it's also possible to address their spiritual wellbeing by:

1. Creating a context, in a world where many have a low sense of self-esteem, enabling people to understand and experience the awesome nature of God; to realise he is not remote and delights in us, as he does the rest of his creation.

2. Offering, in our frenetic and fast paced world, the gift of enabling people to creatively apply the insights from Jesus' life to their own lives by learning how to prioritise; creating pools of stillness via the application of spiritual disciplines.

3. Connecting the importance of breathing exercises, which are a key part of mindfulness, to the way in which God breathed creation into existence, and Jesus breathed the empowering gift of the Holy Spirit upon his disciples on the first Easter Day.

4. Unpacking how aspects of Jesus' teaching connect with aspects of mindfulness. For example, how to be present in the moment; resources for dealing with stress and anxiety; being non-judgemental; self-compassion; awareness of others; enjoying, and finding healing in, creation. Helpful examples are Forest Church and Mindful walks.

5. Learning from Jesus about reimagining church as a safe and spacious place where community is formed, in a non-judgemental context, people can 'be', ask questions, and grow into wholeness and holiness, exploring discipleship in a creative and positive way.

6. Sharing food together in quiet and mindful ways. Jesus loved to eat with his friends and with those who became his friends and followers through eating with him! Eating together can be an antidote to

loneliness, give a deeper appreciation of taste and our other senses, as well as creating a greater thankfulness for God's provision for all our needs - living with an attitude of gratitude.

6 WHAT NEXT FOR YOU?

In this concluding chapter we hope to suggest some potential initiatives you could develop. We want to stress from the outset that we believe every context will be unique - the approach is not linear or a "one size fits all." In some contexts, all suggested models might be utilised and in others just one. We believe that all approaches involve fulfilling some aspect of the principles found in Isaiah 61:1 and Luke 4:18.

Depending on their particular focus and purpose, some of the following initiatives may be deemed as a fresh expression of church, others offer a much-needed addition to what a re-imagined church could offer in its missional engagement. Others may simply be an outworking of the Missio Dei; bringing hope to a hurting world.

A) A local church might, as part of its mission action plan, apply some funding to a local secular mindfulness project where trained mindfulness teachers are offering courses to enable people to better cope with the strains of living in the busyness of the 21st century post pandemic world.

B) A local church might recruit a Christian who is trained in mindfulness to offer secular training in a secular venue, or they pay for a member of the church to train up. No explicit Christian teaching but there would be the opportunity to speak of the ways that their faith enables them to be more mindful.

C) A local church might recruit a Christian who is trained in mindfulness to offer 'secular' training in a church or church building. Again, no explicit Christian teaching but the opportunity to speak of the ways they are mindful through their faith.

D) Building on B or C a mindfulness session or course might have built community between participants. Might they then be offered something which is not specifically Christian but may involve meditating on scripture or alluding to aspects of Christianity. It would be important to be transparent about this in any publicity

E) Building on D a fresh expression might be developed, comprising interested members of the group, specifically based on insights of Christian mindfulness. Reflecting the core values of Fresh Expressions, taken from freshexpressions.org.uk:
Contextual - individuals interested in mindfulness and wanting to explore more about its connections with the Christian faith
Ecclesial - church being formed
Formational - growing together and learning more about Jesus
Missional - growing in their understanding of Jesus and then using the insights of mindfulness to offer further sessions in 'secular' settings

F) As a church - when a few people have had some experience of and training in mindfulness, make connections with local GP practices to explore the possibilities of working in partnership. Such as in the areas of mental health and well-being, with a view to offering mindfulness sessions on their premises.

G) During seasons such as Advent or Lent explore how a Christian application of mindfulness could help address subjects such as: making wise decisions in life, reducing anxiety, work-life balance, coping with temptation and learning to be content in life.

H) Having run mindfulness sessions for members of an existing congregation, under God, discern who from among them has the gifting and passion to be part of a team looking to develop what could become a fresh expression of church, specifically based on the principles of Christian mindfulness. This could be in person and/or online.

It seems to us that, in the spirit of the apostle Paul's experience in the city of Athens (Acts 17: 16-34), these are all part of an intentional commitment to connect with those for whom church is not on their radar, but who are searching for something more in life. In summation, we find that Shaun Lambert articulates this well when he says, "Mindfulness as a human capacity is a collection of jigsaw pieces we can use to make different jigsaw puzzles. The central stand of these puzzles is to do with healing, wholeness, and the transformation of our perceptive faculties. Mindfulness matters for Christians, but not just for us, our neighbours, for God and for creation itself."[24]

---

[24] Shaun Lambert, *What does Mindfulness offer the Christian?* (Article in the Baptist Times, 11/05/2015).

APPENDIX: THE FRESH EXPRESSIONS PRAYER

Gracious God,

Keep us ever mindful of your presence,

Thankful for what has been and excited for what is to come.

May we walk in humility always hungry for more of you.

Open our ears that we would always hear you;

Break our hearts for what hurts you.

Holy Spirit lead us always to where you need us to be;

Equip us to be a courageous movement, telling stories of hope

And proclaiming, in fresh ways, the Good News to this generation;

to the Glory of our Lord and Saviour Jesus Christ.

BIBLIOGRAPHY / SUGGESTED READING

BABBS, L., *Into God's presence: Listening to God through prayer and meditation* (Michigan: Zondervan, 2005).

BELL, R., *How to be here,* n.d.

CASEY, M., *Sacred reading,* (Liguori, Mo.: Liguori/Triumph 2008).

DE CAUSSADE, JEANNE- PIERRE., *Abandonment to Divine Providence,* (Indiana, Ave Maria Press, 2010).

CHESTERSTON, G. *St. Francis of Assisi.* [S.l.]: (Wildside Press 2020).

CRAY, G., MOBSBY, I., KENNEDY, A., ed. *Fresh Expressions and the Kingdom of God* (London Canterbury Press 2012).

COE, J.H., and STROBEL, K.C., ed. *Embracing Contemplation* (Strobel IVP Academic, 2019).

COLLICUTT, J., BRETHERTON, R., BRICKMAN, J., *Being Mindful, Being Christian* (Chicago: Lion Hudson 2016).

DRAPER, B., *Soulfulness* (Hodder & Stoughton Canada 2020).

FRUEHWIRTH, G., *Words for Silence: A Year of Contemplative Meditations* (SPCK, 2008)

KNIGHT, R., *Mission in a Time of Trauma* (Cambridge, Grove Books Ltd, 2021)

MARIONA, J. and WILBER, K., *Putting on the mind of Christ* (Newburyport: Hampton Roads Publishing 201).

MCINTOSH, MARK A., *Mystical theology: The integrity of spirituality and theology* (Blackwell Publishing, 1998).

LAIRD, M., *Into the Silent Land* (London: DLT, 2006).

LAMBERT, S., *A Book of Sparks: A Study in Christian MindFullness* (Watford: Instant Apostle, 2014).

__, *Putting on the wakeful one* (Watford: Instant Apostle, 2016).

LAWRENCE, BR., Lawrence, Br., *The Practice of the presence of God (*Mockingbird Classics, 2015).

LISIEUX, T., *The Autobiography of Thérèse of Lisieux* (Newburyport: Dover Publications, 2012).

MAIN, J., *Being Present Now: Door to Silence* (Norwich: Canterbury Press, 2006).

___, *The Heart of Creation* (London: DLT, 1988).

MOYNAGH, M., *Being Church, Doing Life* (Oxford: Monarch, 2014).

MOYNAGH, M., and BECK, *The 21st Century Christian: Following Jesus Where Life Happens.* (A Fresh Expressions book, 2021).

NATARAJA, K., *Journey to the heart* (Maryknoll, N.Y.: Orbis Books 2012).

NOUWEN, H.J.M., *The Way of the Heart* (New York: Harper Collins, 1981).

ODEN, AMY G., *Right Here, Right Now: The Practice of Christian Mindfulness* (Nashville: Abingdon Press, 2017).

REYNOLDS, S., *Living with the Mind of Christ* (Minneapolis, Minnesota: Augsburg Books 2020).

ROHR, R., *Falling Upward: A Spirituality for the Two Halves of Life* (SPCK, 2012).

STEAD, T., *Mindfulness and Christian Spirituality-Making Space for God* (London: SPCK, 2016).

___, *See, Love, Be: Mindfulness and the Spiritual Life: a practical eight-week guide* (London, SPCK, 2018).

___, *Mindfulness and Prayer* (Cambridge: Grove Books Ltd, 2016).

THOMAS, G., *Sacred pathways* (Grand Rapids, Mich: Zondervan 2000).

WELCH, S., n.d. *How to be a mindful Christian.*

WILLIAMS, M. and PENMAN, d., *Mindfulness: A Practical Guide to Finding Peace in a Frantic World* (London, Piatkus 2011).

Websites

https://cac.org

https://www.churchtimes.co.uk

https://freshexpressions.org.uk

https://www.leeds.anglican.org

http://sanctuaryfirst.org.uk

http://mindandsoul.info

http://shaunlambert.co.uk

http://mindfulnesscds.com

https://sheridanvoysey.com

https://wellbeingjourney.org

https://www.spst.edu

ABOUT THE AUTHORS

Karen Openshaw

Kare runs a consultancy which provides a listening service for organisations and individuals, drawing on the 'toolbox' of her eclectic mix of counselling, mentoring, chaplaincy, and coaching training. She offers coaching for business owners and those with leadership responsibilities. Karen delivers workshops in both Christian and secular organisations, introducing people to the concept of mindfulness. She developed a fresh expression of church in 2012 at the Oasis Academy, Media City UK in Salford, where she was chaplain. She was a board director for Fresh Expressions Ltd from 2017-2020.

Chris Edmondson

Chris has worked in a variety of parish and diocesan posts in the Church of England, as well as having been Warden of Lee Abbey, Devon from 2002 to 2008. Prior to his retirement in 2016, Chris was for eight years Bishop of Bolton in the Diocese of Manchester. During that time, he chaired the Manchester Fresh Expressions Area Strategy Team, and was also Vice Chair of the National Fresh Expressions Board. Chris has been the Chair of the Council of Scargill House since 2009 and is the author of two books on leadership. Having been ordained for almost 50 years, Chris continues to be committed to seeing the Gospel freshly expressed, for each new generation.

Printed in Great Britain
by Amazon